MW01644272

About the Author

My name is Quentoria Brooks, and I was born on August 26, 1991. To Wilsonya Brooks. I am the youngest of three girls. Aretha Brooks the oldest and Lasonya Brooks, who is the middle child. At the age of 4 years old my mother past. Our mother, Mom took us in and raised us. I still have a vague memory of my mother. Like the time when she was crying in pain and couldn't express how bad her head hurt, due to the tumor growing inside her head and my grandmother walking towards her shaking with a glass of ice water to give my mother. The ambulance was called, and that was the last time I had seen her move. When I had to tell her goodbye was the kiss my uncle picked me up to give her on her forehead. She was lying in a pink casket and wearing a pink gown. My grandmother gave me so much love. I didn't feel void from my mother being deceased. My Dad would come around often, but he and my grandmother weren't always on good terms. Raising me wasn't always easy.

I was kicked out of school, so my grandmother thought it might be better for me to go to live with my dad sister, Niecy who had four kids of hers living there as well. I was sexually assaulted by her son and had to see him in school the next day. I felt disgusted. The grunts and looks he would give me pierced me and embarrassed me. My self-esteem was low, and I just wanted to hide my face from everyone. I suffered in silence while smiling when I got around people like everything was okay. I never discuss this till now. And his mother didn't make it any better just because I wasn't her child, she yelled at me for just being there. I would hear her talk about me bad on the phone in the next room. I didn't understand why I was being spoken bad about and treated that way, and I was barely eating. So, I dropped out of school and left, went back to my grandmothers. I have always been a grandmother girl, and I had slept in the same bed as my granny until I was 18 years old. I met who I thought was the love of my life through a mutual friend. My first/Love, we started as a friend, and it progressed into a relationship. We did everything together. I had my first child at 20 years old.

Our relationship went down drain; he was a cheater and abuser. There were times he choked me till I passed out. I was scared and in love. I kept allowing him back in my life. Because I thought he must love me cause each time he would come looking for me and begging me again. Each time it got worse, and I was pregnant the third and last time and said enough is enough. The hope of it getting better was gone so I went and filed a restraining order against him. And, I never looked back. I have three beautiful daughters from him. They are my reasons and strength.

Dear, Reader I want you to understand that you didn't stumble upon this book by accident. It is a divine destiny that you have received this book. It is with love and peace I give you. Understand you are loved and needed here in this life. May your journey be blessed. This book is very personal to me. While I was writing this book, I have guarded and protected it from anyone eyes till now. I hope this book brings you healing as much as it has given me. I was having a difficult time with my break-up at moments while I was writing and through the process, I found myself healing and experiencing a transformation in growth and self-love. I know that patience is essential. Don't rush yourself to become what you think the world is expecting you to be. This is your life. You must live it for yourself. So, take as much time needed for self.

Thank you!

7 Chakras and Healing

A 7 Chakra and Healing Workbook to accelerate self-healing and balance

By

Quentoria Brooks

 The author of this book does not dispense any form of medical or psychologist advice or prescribe the use of any technique as a form of treatment for physical, emotions, or medical problems without the advice of a physician, either directly or indirectly. The author intends to offer information of a general nature to help you in your search for emotional and spiritual well-being. If you apply any of the techniques provided in the book, the author and the publisher assume no responsibility for your actions.

For more information about this Author
Instagram/iamquentoriab
quentoria.brooks@yahoo.com

Chapter 1

What are Chakras

The 7 Chakras are the seven centers of spiritual power in the human body. Each chakra corresponds with a different organ in your body. The physical, mental, phycological states of conscious being, they govern various emotional issues, from our survival instincts and self-esteem to our ability to communicate and experience love. Chakras can become blocked through an emotional upset, such as conflict, loss, or accident. Fear, anxiety, and stress are common causes of chakra imbalances. It is these blocks that disrupt the harmony and eventually causes disease, emotional and mental disorders in the physical body. When they are open and align, they are in the state of balance and flow. I will be giving details on how to know when your chakra could be blocked, imbalanced, overactive and how it could be affecting your life. Also, how to open and balance your chakras. There are seven chakras: the root chakra, the sacral chakra, the solar plexus chakra, the heart chakra, the throat chakra, the third eye chakra, and the crown chakra. Each chakra is possessing its color and vibrational frequency. Everything in the universe is all about balance and aligning. Everything vibrates at its own frequency.

Root Chakra

The Root chakra is the first chakra it is located at the base of the spine. The color of this chakra is red. The element is earth. Represents our foundation on which we build our life, safety, security, stability and feeling of being grounded. When this chakra is overactive, it leads to the greed of power and materialism. When this chakra is blocked the attributes would be having a lot of fears, anxiety can easily infiltrate your thoughts, making everything suddenly feel uncertain. And you may have hard times concentrating and worrying about your well-being. Which can manifest paranoia, physical issues caused by a blocked root chakra include a sore lower back, low energy level, and pain in the legs, when this chakra is opened and balance you feel grounded, at ease with fewer worries and less fear. The physical body regains its strength and stamina. And your basic sense of stability that you develop will permeate all aspects of your life. There are ways of opening and balancing the root chakra. Like spending time in nature, taking walks in the park or taking your bare feet placing it on the earth's surface. Also influencing the root chakra to open and balance by using stones like; Red Jasper, this stone is linked to balancing energy. It often leads to independence and spontaneous leadership. Red carnelian, it is associated with strength, cleansing, bravery, and motivation. Obsidian, it is said to protect you from harm, it blocks a psychic attack and absorbs negative energies from the environment. Bloodstone, it is linked to pushing away negative energy and increase confidence; it is an energy cleanser. The yoga position is the balasana, which involves lying face down, resting on your knees and calves, then extending your arms out in front of you as your head drops down between them. These chakra foods are protein-rich foods, vegetables and spices like; beans, tofu, green peas, spinach, eggs, beets, onions, carrot, potatoes, parsnips, chives, and pepper. The affirmation to say for your root chakra is entirely up to you but here are some suggested assertions.

Wherever I am, I am safe and secured

I am secure and happy with who I am

I am one with the universe

I have a healthy mind and a healthy body

I am stable

I deserve and receive support whenever I need it

Sacral Chakra

The Sacral chakra is the second chakra it is located, in the middle of the abdomen, roughly two inches below the navel. The color of this chakra is orange. The element is water. The foundation of this chakra is creativity and sexuality. When this chakra is overactive, it causes sexual addiction, manipulation, and self-fulfillment. When this chakra is blocked, the attributes would be lack of creativity, Boredom, jealousy, emotional isolation, OCD, uninspired, feelings of guilt, feeling easily offended, fear of change, low-self-worth, sexual dysfunction, and with-held intimacy. Which can manifest low energy and reduce Physical libido issues caused by a blocked sacral chakra includes urinary discomfort and attraction to addictive behaviors. When this chakra is opened and balance you have feelings of passion and openness. Having fulfillment and creativity. Also, when this chakra is open and balances it gives you the confidence to make significant changes to the way you live your life. There are ways to open and balance the sacral chakra. Like camping being outside under the mood light, being around open water or dancing. Also influencing the sacral chakra to open and restore by using stones like; Orange calcite is said to enhance creativity, help you move past emotional blocks. Moonstone is supposed to reduce worry, balancing hormones and providing support during periods of hormonal change such as puberty or menopause. Carnelian is said to give off powerful energy, reduce tension and stress. It helps to harmonize with the environment and people. Citrine is supposed to increase self-esteem and stimulates mental power and helps you to focus. The yoga position for this chakra is the goddess pose. Begin standing up straight with your arms at your sides. Bring your hands to rest comfortably on your hips.

Turn to the right and step your feet wide apart, about four feet. Turn your toes out slightly, so they point outward. Bend your knees and lower your hip into a squat. Bring your thighs parallel to the floor do not force yourself into a squat. Extend your arms out to the sides at shoulder-height with your palms facing down. Then, spiral your thumbs up towards the ceiling, your upper arms and forearms should be at a 90-degree angle. These chakra foods are oranges, seeds, coconuts, and teas. The affirmations to say for your sacral chakra is entirely up to you but here are some suggested assertions.

I am open to what the universe has in store for me
I am fulfilled every day I experience the joy
I am passionate and full of inspiration
I am ready for positive change and personal growth

Solar Plexus Chakra

The Solar Plexus chakra is the third chakra it is located just below your chest in between your navel and rib cage. The color of this chakra is yellow. The element is fire. The foundation of this chakra is wisdom, pleasure, and power. When this chakra is overactive, the results are being too critical, being power hungry, and having control issues. When this chakra is blocked, the attributes are lack of direction, low self-esteem, indecisiveness, misuse of power, shame, victim mentality, feeling helpless, unresolved guilt about the past and feeling like you need to control everything and everyone around you. Block solar plexus can also manifest difficulties in relationships with others. The physical issues caused by a blocked solar plexus chakra include problems with memory, nausea, and digestive cramps.

When this chakra is open and balances you are driven, ambitious, confidence and a positive self-image. There are ways to open and balance this chakra like; Doing belly breaths and being in the sunlight. Also influencing the solar plexus chakra to open and restore by using stones like; Amber it links to mental clarity and self-confidence. Yellow tourmaline is said to promote a healthy mood. Citrine is supposed to increase self-esteem and stimulates spiritual power and helps you to focus. The yoga position for this chakra is the warrior pose. Stand straight up, lightly jump your feet 31/2 to 4 feet apart. Raise your arms perpendicular to the floor (and parallel to each other) and reach toward the ceiling. This chakra foods are yellow pepper, corn, and chamomile tea. The affirmations to say for your solar plexus chakra is entirely up to you but here are some suggested assertions.

I am the embodiment of love and inner peace

I am confident

I feel motivated to pursue my purpose

I am ambitious

Chapter 2

Heart Chakra

The Heart chakra is the fourth chakra it is located, in the center of the chest. The color of this chakra is green. The element is air. The foundation of this chakra is when your physical and spiritual needs met, awareness, love, and healing. When this chakra is an overactive feeling of codependence, lack of trust, jealousy, over apologizing and self-sacrificing. When this chakra is blocked, the attributes would be restlessness, impatience, irritability, grief, hatred and belief issues. Blocked heart chakra can also manifest relationship difficulties with others. The physical problems caused by a blocked heart chakra is increasing in blood pressure, insomnia, and disease in immune system function. When this chakra is open and balance you have feelings of love and compassion, peace, and high vibration. There are ways to open and balance this chakra like; Being out in nature, spending time with children and animals. Also influencing the heart chakra to open and restore by using stones like; Jade it is said to help when dealing with loss and balancing. Green calcite its benefits are absorbing negative energy and encourages forgiveness of oneself and others and brings softness to the heart, stimulating compassion. Green aventurine is said to soothe difficult emotions. Rose quartz is said to regain balance. The yoga position for this chakra is the camel pose. Lean back with chin tilt up and head back. With the bending of your back, while your hands are touching your ankles. These chakra foods are spinach, kale, limes, green apples, soups, food rich in vitamin c. The affirmations to say for your heart chakra is entirely up to you but here are some suggested assertions.

I love myself unconditionally

I am open to love

My heart chakra is open

I am passionate

I am one with the universe and all that dwells within

Throat Chakra

The throat chakra is the fifth chakra it is located, in the center of your neck. The color if this chakra is blue. The element is Ether. The foundation of this chakra is communication, truth, and self-expression. When this chakra is overactive, you become rude being very loud, using harsh words, being opinionated, interrupting and gossiping. When this chakra is blocked the attributes are lack of attention, lack of focus and dishonesty. Blocked throat chakra can also manifest inability to say what you want to say. The physical issues caused by a blocked throat chakra is a sore throat, a stiff or achy neck. When this chakra is open and balance it is excellent communication skills, speaking the truth and good listening skills. There are ways to open and balance this chakra like; by writing, start a journal. Also influencing the throat chakra to open and restore by using stones like; Lapus lazuli it is often called "stone of truth" it helps with communication and honesty. Aquamarine represents courage and acceptance. Amazonite protects you against negativity. Turquoise helps to boost confidence in contact. The yoga position for this chakra is sitting quietly on a meditation mat or in a chair and focusing on your throat. As you are breathing in relax, and while breathing out with humming. Continue for 5 minutes. It is supported to do this exercise daily or at least three times a week. These chakra foods are blueberries, fruits that grow on trees, lemongrass and ginger. The affirmations to say for your throat chakra is entirely up to you but here are some suggested assertions.

I am an excellent communicator with good listening skills

I speak my truth

My voice is important, and others understand me

Third Eye Chakra

The third eye chakra is the sixth chakra it is located, in the center of the forehead, between the eyebrows. The color of this chakra is indigo. The element is Extra-Sensory perception. The foundation of this chakra is awareness, intuition, wisdom, and insight. When this chakra is overactive, you have trouble sleeping, bad nightmares, obsessiveness, hallucinations, inability to make good decisions, feel clumsy, and learning disorder. When this chakra is blocked cause lack of imagination, poor judgment, and struggle with faith. A blocked third eye chakra can also manifest poor decisions. The physical issues caused by a blocked third eye chakra are headaches (including migraines), sinus and eye discomfort. When this chakra is open, and balance is intuition, clear vision, and clear thoughts. There are ways to open and balance this chakra like; starting a dream journal. Also influencing the third eye chakra to open and restore by using stones like; Purple fluorite it is said to help with making difficult choices and get rid of irrelevant distractions. Amethyst helps with headache relief. Black obsidian promotes a balance between emotion and reason. The yoga position for this chakra is the downward dog. Begin on your knees. Stretch your elbows and relax your upper back. Spread your fingers wide and press firmly through your palm's knuckles. Exhale as you tuck your toes and lift your knees off the floor. Press the floor away from you as you raise your pelvis. This chakra foods are dark chocolate, eggplant, purple cabbage, red grapes, blueberries, blackberries, walnuts, salmon, and sardines. The affirmations to say for your third eye chakra is entirely up to you but here are some suggested assertions.

I always make the right decisions to benefit my well being

I have unlimited possibilities available

I am confident

I trust my intuition

Crown Chakra

The crown chakra is the seventh chakra is located, at the top of your head. The color of this chakra is violet. The element is thought. The foundation of this chakra is spirituality and connection to your higher self. When this chakra is overactive is obsessiveness, isolation, judgmental, and dogmatic. When this chakra is blocked you experience symptoms of depression, anxiety, disconnection, self-destructive tendencies, cynicism and learning difficulties. A blocked crown chakra can also manifest chronic headaches. The physical issues that are caused by a blocked crown chakra are chronic problems. When this chakra is an open and balanced feeling of awareness, universal love, faith, understanding, wisdom, your ability to find peace, self-worth, and alignment. There are ways to open and balance this chakra like; you can sit 10 to 15 in the silence of meditation. Also influencing the crown chakra to open and balance by using stones like; Clear quartz you use clear quartz to boost your spiritual attunement. Sugilite is used to support spiritual grounding and for guarding you against negativity. Selenite it is said to help open not only the crown chakra but also the third eye chakra, it helps in pushing you past stagnation and in propelling you forward. The yoga position for this chakra is the headstand and or silent or guided meditation for 10 to 15 minutes. These chakra foods are red grapes, ginger, herbal teas. The affirmations to say for this chakra are entirely up to you but here are some suggested assertions.

I see beauty in the world, and I embrace it

I am confident, happy and sure of my worth

Today I am open to divine guidance

I am complete

I am worthy of love and divine energy

Chapter 3

Welcome to Healing

Welcome to healing is the second topic in this book because we have all had to overcome adversity, in your past or you may be going through trouble right now in this present moment. I could tell you many experiences I've had and got through them. I know what it is like feeling depressed like you have failed. Times I was heartbroken from not having the person I love there with me, feeling desperate, deserted and lonely. Questioning myself a lot and thinking I wasn't good enough. I knew those feelings way to well. Overcoming my adversities, I can say honestly, I gained patience and so much love and respect for myself. I have gotten stronger. And you will get through it too. You will increase so much self-love and strength. Be strong and of good courage in this time because you are not alone. The Lord your God, He is the one who goes with you. He will not leave nor forsake you. If this were not true, I would not tell you. Be patient with yourself; being patient with yourself is love. People tend to say, love yourself, but they forget to mention to you even while you're hurting and going through pain from adversity love yourself. Love is long-suffering but, never fails. Know that God is with you every step of the way. I knew I wanted out of the emotional misery I felt. My thoughts at the time kept me in the state of hurting. I was drained, and I cried many nights. I would call my cousin and talk to her about what I was going through. It never helped the situation just gave it attention. I just needed someone to vent to, and she was a listening ear. Then I stop calling her about it and started writing everything on paper about what I was going through, and I just kept giving it more attention. Till one day I notice the more I brought attention to it the more I would feel the hurt and betrayal from it all over again. Emotions I no longer wanted to explore. I Decided to try something new, so I wrote down the feelings of what I felt was happiness and what I wanted to feel. I wrote "I am so happy with the way my life is going. I met the love of my life, and he gives me all the love and attention I want. I smile every day knowing my family is supportive of me. I have so much money, and I love my career. I am blessed. I thank God.

Once I started a thought of what I want, other thoughts came to mind, and my emotions began to change. I wasn't having feelings of disappointment, loss or desperation anymore. I would write and read them daily till I memorized them so that it would become a belief subconsciously. And, I would repeat them to myself while I'm going about my day. The feeling was blissful and satisfying to say the lease. I learned if you are going through adversity the way to get out of that current state of being is to think out, by thinking of what you want. The one wanting thought creates other thoughts of wanting. You don't need to complain every 2 to 3 minutes about what you are going through or what you don't like or want. At that present moment that is already the state of being you are in. You put too much energy around that unwanted situation by complaining and talking about it and making it grow and giving you more of those adverse issues. Think of your thoughts as seeds and your emotions as the water and your spoken words as the sun. You will bring growth to whatever you give rain and sun too. Do not talk about what is not wanted. Try to focus on what is desired. Words are creative. They create emotion. I can say the word "Love" and each person that hears it would get a different feeling from that word. Because some people have had bad experiences thinking about love hurts, and some have good experiences and met the love of their lives.

Each time that you speak, there is an emotion behind a word, but you may have never noticed it. Each word vibrates at its own frequency. The frequency of the words we use daily are patterns which we humans are prone to because we are habitual creatures. That's why addictions are so prevalent in this day and time. And, the one way to brake and obsession is to vibrate at a different frequency from your old patterns. The universe feeds off our energy, it is alive and will give you back that which you put in its energy fields, because like attracts like. Once we change the emotion behind our words our life begins to shift. Depending on the words you choose to speak in your life could either be good or a bad shift. The tongue has the power over life and death.

When you want to feel better from feeling sad, use words to uplift your spirit and listen to some music that gets your energy level high that causes you to dance, smile and feel happy. I use affirmation to speak out loud or to myself. "So shall my word be that goes forth out of my mouth; it shall not return unto me void, but it shall accomplish that which I please, and it shall prosper in the thing whereto I sent it." Isaiah 55:11.

I affirm to myself that 'I Am Great, I Am Beautiful, I Am Love, I Am Successful. You can use whatever words that makes you feel good and by putting I Am in front of the statement is affirming a declaration of your truth of who you are or want to become. The feeling from the words starts to register with your subconsciousness. You're saying you are that which you say you are. Your subconscious mind is part of your mind in which you may or may not be fully aware of but influences your actions and feelings. Everyday! So, as you continue to say your affirmation daily, you will start to vibrate on the frequency of that you are because the emotions you put behind your words. Make sure you feel good while saying it. So, I suggest you get yourself in a good mood first. You are the creator of your reality. Creation begins with you.

Chapter 4

Manifesting

Manifesting is our gift from God. And, the world today is evidence of that gift. Manifesting is a physical display of someone's true intention that is done purposely or by default. When you manifest by default, it is still your truths, being displayed. And, with you not wanting them displayed, thoughts that you have inward with the added emotions creates default manifesting. Default manifested experiences are the truth about how you feel about yourself and or others. A single thought will bring about other similar ideas. When you combine thought with an emotion you will manifest the experience. Positive thinking and negative emotions will get you zero results of what your wanting and negative thought and positive emotion will get you zero results of what you are wanting. Because you will get a result you are not wanting, and you manifest the experience by default. You cannot fake a positive thought or emotion. It just won't work. That which you want you can manifest it in your life. But manifesting is not prejudice to any persons or situation. It works the same all the time. That which you want you, do get, and that which you don't want you, do get because both have emotions behind the craving and not wanting from the words you speak when saying the wanting and not wanting. In this book, you will have a clear understanding of Being. The existence of which you are right now. In hopes that in the reading of this book you will examine yourself. And in that examination, you would understand what caused the outcomes of your experiences. And how you can change the result of your life experiences. How you can get exactly what you want. This work is put forth for the good of humankind. No form of misleading is in this written book. Before getting started, I also must inform you that nothing happens overnight. But with faith and works being applied consistently all things are possible, and you will receive exactly. I firmly believe that we experience life from what we have thought about. It was a thought that came about first. The pattern of that thought being of consistency become manifested in the physical through actions, people and experiences. Nothing can be placed in our life without us accepting it consciously or subconsciously.

We create our reality. We are powerful beings, anything we want we can have. We do not lack anything. We are whole and complete. God made us perfect in his image. We have free-will, and mistakes or past experiences do not hinder you. Forgiveness is love and Love keeps no records of wrongs. God is Love. And you are loved.

Ownership

This is a personal topic for everyone. Because it's a mirror for you to look at "YOU". Ownership, the act. What we do when something happens. We react right? Well based upon that reaction other events will take place. It is that cause and effect scenario. Like how "the alarm clock goes off and wakes you up." So, when there is a situation an if that event occurred was a disagreement with arguing and fussing between two or more people. Based on your reaction, responding to the event happening with yelling and arguing back at the person/persons. You accepted that adverse outcome because you return with actions or word in response. As I said before nothing can be placed in your life without you allowing it. When you react to something negative, you accepted. And it is telling the universe you like negativity because the world goes off reaction, and attraction. So, it brings more of the adverse events that occur at certain times because negativity vibrates at a certain frequency. A particular word can spark an emotion for the negative frequency in actions and events. Hearing Gossip, going to certain places, a specific song, watching certain shows. There are many thought triggers to spark that emotion to manifest into your life experience. The same goes for positive experiences. Being appreciative of everything you already have. Focusing on what makes you happy. Being kind to everyone. Accepting and loving yourself, people and all that's around you, are very positive and brings more positivity in your life. Energy is transferable. When we interact with sad people. And if you are talking with them trying to cheer them up, the energy transfer to you and caused you to feel empathy.

May even bring up old feelings you've had before. So being careful with who and what you allow in is essential for your happiness. The frequency is different with each energy. Do you know the frequency you are vibrating on? Most people don't. But that doesn't mean you can't find out. Remember the old saying when your mom, grandmother, aunt or dad used to say, "show me your friends and I'll show you your future." That scenario remains today. You must want more for yourself to get what you want in life. When you take ownership of the way, you have been responding to life, Your life! That it has been you all along doing those things that caused your experiences. No one else "just you." They probably influence you, because of the vibrational frequency that you both are vibrating on. "As iron sharpens iron, so one man sharpens another" Proverbs 27:17. So blaming someone for the way you react and respond has nothing at all to do with them but so much to do with yourself.

Vibration Frequency

Everything in the universe is made up of energy vibrating at different frequencies. Even things that look solid from a physical aspect are made up of vibrational energy fields at the quantum level. This includes you. All vibrations operate at high and low frequencies, with us and around us. And the universe feeds off those frequencies and gives us more of what our level of vibrational frequency is. We have all responded negatively to a situation more than once, and once was to many because it told the universe that you will react if it gives you more negativity. Like attracts like. Remember when I said words have emotion behind them, well it's also energy. You can say a word with hatred. And it will mean one thing. And say that same word with love, and it will mean something different. So, you will get two different emotions and reactions depending on how you say it and feel when saying it. I am going to show you a way to find out your vibrational frequency. I have seven questions I want you to answer. Doing this will bring acknowledgment to either a positive or negative vibrational frequency level you are vibrating on

Do not get offended because nothing is set in stone doing this VF chart. I created it to help get myself and others vibrational level. Anything can be changed that is not wanted if you feel like you are stuck in that same situation or keep repeating those same mistakes. That's a cycle, and until you change your vibrational frequency, you will continue to vibrate on that frequency. Knowledge is power.

Vibrational Frequency Chart:
Root Chakra- Do you have anxiety about work, relationships and life in general, like you don't know what to do?
Sacral Chakra- Do you feel a lack of interest in intimacy and emotional isolation?
Solar Plexus Chakra- Do you have a problem with self-esteem but want to be in control and sometimes can be manipulative?

Heart Chakra- Do you have depression at times and lack of self-discipline?
Throat Chakra- Do you feel withdrawn at times and shyness?
Third Eye Chakra- Do you feel like sometimes you don't know what to do or have the clarity to think clearly to decide?
Crown Chakra- Do you argue a lot and think your right most of the time being close-minded?

A yes answer to 1 or more question still requires attention. There is an ole saying how one apple spoiled the whole batch. This is not the if it isn't broke do not fix it type of situation, this is your life, your peace and your experience in being so if any of your answers are yes and includes an explanation. It means your acknowledgment is present, but your denial is also current. Stop playing tug of war with your being. Your Vibrational Frequency is low and has a negative energy frequency. Negative energy frequencies are connected to Negative experiences and people you know or met in your life.

By having the negative frequency all, it will take is just one negative thought to manifest something you don't want. And If you don't change that. That is what you will continue getting. The explanations of your reasons are the excuses to keep going about that way. You may have a good job but having a wrong time in your relationships, or no job and good relationships. That is when something in your energy frequency is throwing off your balance, for you to have that love you want to have. The money you want to have. And whatever else it is you are wanting to align yourself to the things that you are wanting. You must evaluate the things you are wanting by writing them down.

What do you want?
Why do you want what you are wanting?
Do you feel you deserve what you are wanting?

What motion of action towards your wants are you going to take physically to achieve that which you are wanting?
Affirmation for what you are wanting?

I like to write my wants down, and right beside the desires, I write my action towards my wants, and then I write down some affirmations to get me in a positive mindset for the achieving and receiving of my desires. It also gives me more clarity when I write them down. It is essential that you focus on the state that you want instead of the country that you are currently in. What are you affirming to yourself is a big part of getting what you want? When you feel like you're in deep water, don't allow that state of being in that current situation stop you from the act of faith, know that you will not be in that situation for long because the action you are taking today will put forth the work towards your faith. Faith alone does not get results of what you are wanting. It is said that "Faith without Works is Dead" James 2:14-26. Faith will work together with your works and by works faith is made perfect. Think as if you're out of that situation already. Faith tells us although physically we cannot see it nor touch it, our belief tells us it's real, so we believe. If you keep allowing yourself to think in the current state that you're in, you will continue to be in that state because there is a law that says. What you think about you bring about. An anything that is thrown in the water and if it's heavy enough it's going to sink deeper. But if you allow yourself to rise, you can float on top of that water, and that's overcoming your trials and tribulations so don't allow your past to be your present. We're all looking for that aha moment. Well, I hope that this book gives you a "thought" and with that thought, I hope that thought gives you motivation and, in that motivation, I hope it gives you action an in that action I hope you change your life for the good.

Chapter 5

You Are Beyond the physical

You are so much more than a physical being. You are not just a body with a spirit, but you are a spirit with a body. We create from the inside out into the universe. I am the creator of my reality whatever I focus on in thought I create. Sometimes we create by default. How you create by default is to think of something. And the emotion you feel while you're thinking that thought. Then the other thoughts that are created from that first thought, it manifests into physical form or experience. Manifesting is part of our everyday lives. Some people know what it is but don't know how to use it. Other uses it but afraid to give the real knowledge behind it and the rest don't know what it is at all. But I am here to tell you in detail knowledge I received. First, the thought with added emotion after that comes more similar feel to the first one thought = Manifestation. I only described it twice, so you will get the importance of your thoughts and how you manifest. Some experiences you have had you didn't want, but you manifested them by default. For it is written "Be careful what you think because your thoughts run your life" Proverbs 4:24.

How you manifested those wrong Relationships

When you meet people and get an instant connection. It is because you are vibrating at the same frequency level. Everyone is different and unique; no two persons are the same. Who you fall in love with is your choice, but I have some tips for you to avoid what you don't want So, let me give you an example let's say you are single, and you are wanting a relationship you are talking to family and friends about it, and you say, "I want a relationship, but I don't want a cheater or a liar". Time goes by one day you're out running errands, and this guy or girl approaches you. You strike up a good conversation, you both connect. Being on the same vibrational frequency. You both started dating.

The relationship goes on for a couple of months; then, you find out he or she is cheating, and you confront them and found out a lot including lies also. Well, you asked for that! You both being co-creators at that time. While you were saying "I want a relationship, but I don't want a cheater or liar" you added emotions while saying those words. And he or she is your co-creator to fulfill that manifestation you created by default. See manifestation works all the time. It gives you what you want and what you don't want. I haven't met anyone yet who didn't say they don't want a cheater or liar and didn't meet the person months later or sooner. My tips are since you are creating your reality, you may as well do it purposely. Have someone ever asked you what your purpose is? Well, what is your goal! Have a goal that is based on your happiness and wants. To manifest the life, people and places you want. Write down what you want in your Significant other. Listening to love songs while doing your writing and envision yourself meeting this person you are wanting. Smile while thinking about it. Put as much love emotion and good feeling behind doing this. You can do this exercise for whatever it is you want, as I said before manifesting is not prejudice to any situation or persons. You will get what you want. And Do not think about what is not desired.

Chapter 6

Self-awareness and Self-motivation

Conscious knowledge of your feelings, motives, and desires. Through adversity, it led you to great self-awareness. I used to think that being in a relationship makes a person happy. But as I have grown up, I have seen that lots of people are in a relationship that they don't want to be in and are not happy. They are just there to have someone next to them at night. When I was in a relationship, I expected too much from him and wondered why I was always disappointed. I was so naive. I thank God for my growth and ability to leave and never return to an old lover. I learned when you let someone else control your happiness. You are setting yourself up for hurt feelings and a broken heart. It's the control of your pleasure, not the other persons. They are just a part of it. And with or without them you still should be happy with yourself. Expectations from others can lead to disappointments.
Disappointments lead to self-doubt. Self-doubt will

have you feeling as if you don't have any control of anything. When we focus on ourselves, it gives us self-worth. I always write it is very therapeutic to me. So, I write down five things I love and appreciate and five things that make me happy. This exercise is for you to focus on what makes you happy. This is your life; no one else can live this life for you. Here is an affirmation that you can say to yourself and believe it.

Affirmation of Thinking:

I choose happiness from this day forward. My peace is essential to me; my understanding is clear to me. I have fought the fight, and I have won, I come out on top. The reward is for me. I have the victory of clarification, and I have the triumph of confirmation. That I am successful, That I am prosperous, That I am victorious. There is no battle anymore because I have already won the prize and the prize is ME. The peace I have it's like a cool breeze in the summer time. The understanding I have it's like a clear blue sky. The love that I have is eternal without convenience nor limitations. I am pure me, and I accept my uniqueness and greatness. All my thoughts work for me and all the results I get from my thoughts I love and appreciate. I am happy every day of my life. I will continue to be joyful and prosperous.

Chapter 7

Limitations and your beliefs

Don't let restrictions stop your belief. You only go as far as you allow your thoughts to take you. Your thinking controls the outcome of your life experiences with people and events. When someone asks, "what rights you have! You must do this to receive that". You reply, "My free will, is my right." We were created to have dominion over the earth. But because we have a society that set limits to our beliefs. So, when you say I want a million dollars. And I suppose that it is already yours just vibrate at the frequency to receive your million dollars. But your friends and family say to you well, you must work hard to earn a million dollars, and that is a 1% chance out of 5 million that you will receive that. They are allowing their beliefs from what they have been taught by society to limit them from accepting what is already theirs, to begin with. You must choose to live on your own free will, which is your birthright or continue to allow others to make you believe things are impossible. Beliefs can either stop you or push you forward in pursuing what it is you want. Some of us have heard of vision boards, and for those that have not, I will give a brief description. It is a collage of images and words representing a person's wishes and goals, intended to serve as inspiration or motivation. But, creations of a new day are the mental work you will do. For example, when you have an appointment the next day. You map out in your head the events. Like you know the route to take to go to the meeting. The exact door to go in and whom to talk to when you arrive. This exercise I have also created for myself that you could use. You are mapping out and organizing the events you want to take place the next day from the day you are right now. Let's say I want a future day to go well tomorrow and to receive good news. I would map out all the things I plan to do, and, in each event, I will envision it going in my favor. I am creating ahead all that I want.

Chapter 8

Perfect love drives out fears

Let me tell you about this couple by the name of "Alexander," they were married and still are. Here is their story. They met in 1991, the year I was born. They were both young. The female whose name was Alex and the male Alexander. They became close friends after a couple of months. Then, their relationship gradually progress. And as they began to know one another beyond the physical. There doubt and insecurities started to reflect on one another. They would fuss and bicker at one another. One day Alexander said to Alex what is your problem. She told you to doubt me, and I am insecure. He told her, that is the way that I feel. After talking they both prayed and fell in a deep sleep. The next morning they'd woken from sleep they looked different to one another. Alex saw herself when she looked at Alexander, and Alexander saw himself when he looked at Alex. That was amusing to them. So, they went about their day. A neighbor called Alex name, and, both answered. The neighbor found it odd. It happened all the time, but they didn't bother to question. See the moral of this story is you feed off one another in relationships; there is no right or wrong; there is only understanding. With them loving themselves it reflected on one another. They became so in love that they started looking alike and answered by one name. Their love persevered, they were one. They became one, and they learned although their doubts and insecurities showed with each other, them having perfect love it drove out those fears. They have been happily married 28 years and counting.

Chapter 9

Universal Responds to your Response

When you respond with words and actions. With emotion behind your response. And if that response is with a feeling of anger and or love. That response has a vibrational frequency, and that energy you give off must come back to you. That is why when your warm and loving to someone, they become open with acceptance to you with a welcoming smile. Energy is transferable. One positive person can't be around negative people; it is either going to cause that person to, leave from around them or absorb that negative energy and, start feeling negative also at that moment. It will create the thought of something negative, which will bring you more relating thoughts from that one thought. Then manifests into an experience. Like when you listen to music that is positive uplifting you get in a positive mood. And when you listen to sad provoking music, you get thought of sadness and may provoke you to address an issue you have with someone. Learning to know what you are allowing in your life does not give you room for error. You can't hang around negative people and expect not to have drama in your life, which brings to accumulate more negative experiences.

Chapter 10

Being

The being of, who you are. The, I am to who you are. We have a clear subconscious mind that we use to see a vision clearly before it manifests into the physical realm, and if we want it with emotion behind that in which we wish to, it becomes a belief subconsciously and will manifest. We all want to be a certain way or seen a certain way. And we can very much so become any way we want to become. That's if you put work behind that faith of wanting and knowing to grow that which you want to become. Let me talk more in-depth with you on the being itself, ourselves. The conscious mind that is how I respond to you and you respond to me through deliberate action and how we choose to think consciously. The subconscious mind that’s our spirit in being, its where all our beliefs are formed. So, we have two minds the conscious mind is what we use to respond for physical, and our subconscious mind is what we use to meet for spiritual and beliefs we have. We are giving those two based on life. That's how life is, and you can't have one without the other. It's like the yin and yang. And when we want to manifest something, we must put our subconscious mind into work, rather than our conscious mind. Because our conscious mind will tell us all the things that society has taught us to believe, that is our limitation. The subconscious mind is our will in being, to do whatever we want to. But, based on what society have taught us our conscious is going to tell us, "No, because hey if you do this. That will not happen for you, or you can't do that because there's a 1% chance out of 3 million that will happen for you". So, we must put our subconscious mind into work when we want something. It is not about consciously what you know, it is about what you believe subconsciously. A person with no education of social teachings, their will power will get them farther because their belief subconsciously that they can and will allow them to receive what they are wanting.

What are you saying to yourself inward, because it is showing outward, and what are your beliefs? Are they limiting you from moving forward in life, is it out of fear that you are stuck in that relationship or job? Fear is mental enslavement. It's not about what the world is doing. Too many people are battling

themselves, trying to prove themselves worthy to others but I say, "you are already worthy."
Stop looking for that hero to save you. Be your hero. When you think out of fear, it comes from your conscious mind from what you have been taught. When God created man, he gave us free will. But, living in the world ruled by governments and dictatorship. They gave laws and limitations to suppress the people so that people can't use power God-given. The free will. They provide education and tell you, you must learn what they are teaching because of its law, and you will be punished or not be anyone in life. But it is a tactic in brainwashing for their purpose of suppression. Because with God free will tells us anything we want we can have. "Ask, and it will be given to you; seek and you will find; knock and the door will be opened to you" Matthew 7:7. Society is telling you all the things that you can't do and having control of things they allow you to do. Only for a fee or your valuable time being spend years trying to accomplish a degree, and once you receive it. You either don't want that career anymore or years later realized that it was not what you are meant to do. We tend to be so hard on ourselves

because we want to live up to a certain expectation, that is expected to live by. Trying to please others is punishment for yourself. It is so many things that have been placed in my heart to tell you. The thought you have about your life is your will of destiny. You are creating your paths with your thoughts you think. The men and women that are out here killing because they don't know, the value of their life. They have no regard for others life. The people who are afraid for their life and manifesting the path of experiencing death by accident or killed by persons that have no respect for their survival. You become co-creators.

Like someone that wants something so strongly and consciously thinks about it, becoming a belief subconsciously and the other person that doesn't want that same thing but, not wanting it actively and is consistently thinking of it and becoming also a belief subconsciously. It manifests for one out of fear, the other out of wanting and preparing. By buying of weapons and being emotionally angry and they are both co-creators of their destiny. A concern is the emotions and thoughts of that fear will manifest. You don't need to think that your life is out of control when you face adversity. Some memories of your past caused unforgiveness and no closure to the situation. There is never closure, and there is only forgiveness of oneself and others. Once you forgive your self, it is so easy to overlook someone else. God is the God of love.

And, love keeps no record of your wrongs, not the God of punishment. So why do you? Why do you punish yourself, when once you have repented from sin? Why revisit with thought and keep that memory of record, of the wrong you have done, and someone else has done to you. You hold on to old emotions that you keep reusing when something reminds you of an experience because you have not forgiven yourself. You must let go of that old thought pattern and forgive yourself. Creating your life experience is how you think your life is going that is the direction you are headed. When you are concerned about your life, and once that thought of concern come about it creates other ideas of fear in other areas of your life like money, relationship, and health. That one thought triggered all these thoughts of concern. Then you start being unsure of yourself and becoming doubtful and with the emotion of anxiety. You will manifest an experience for your interests. I want people to understand how valuable they are. The power they have and the absolute control they have of their life and, live their life better. To know your life is not based on what or how somebody has done to you or what you have done to someone else. No one hinders you but you. By thinking thoughts that limit you and, that have been given you reasons why not to go after what you want in life. I am asking you what do you want? And how are you going after what you are wanting? When you want something, you think just because you want it that means you will one day receive it. But, that's not necessarily true.

Don't let that one-day mindset make you comfortable. I remember being told if I see a shooting star make a wish and it will come true, and I also remember being told one I blow my birthday candles out my wish will come true. Well, I can honestly say I was being told lies. And those same lies kept me wanting but, I was thinking in that one-day mindset. You must put action behind that which you are wanting. So, I got myself in a right frame of thought after meditating for 10 minutes, I sat and mapped out what it is I want, the action I must take for receiving what I want and believing I will accept what I want because I deserve it. The energy I put behind what I want is positive thoughts of me achieving my wants and affirming to myself daily.

I believe that anything I want I can have. Because I am powerful, and I use my power for the good of my being. Feel good in what you wish to don't doubt for a second. Don't talk of words that will work against what you are wanting. Be in one direction with your wanting. Try not to be scattered in decision making. For example, let's say you want to start a business. You would first think of what you want to sale. Find a vendor or way to create your item. Think of a name for your business. Get your business name copyrighted or trademarked. Create a website. Create content. Depending on your social site you choose to find your target audience. Once your social site and content is created, get a budget on advertising. Know how much you are willing to spend, then start advertising, promote yourself and business as much as possible. It is not hard when you believe you can do it. I see so many people read books on how to think like a millionaire or how to think as successful people think. And, I am not knocking those strategies, but I feel you should think like you're thinking but better. Learn to critique your thought you believe in working for you and not against you. You will never think like how someone else thinks because everyone has their way of thinking.

But what I do know those successful people started where you are right now, and they believed they could and did. It only takes that one thought to shift your mind and mood. You can't assume everyone with you; some people will not believe it until you show them. The nay Sayers always get proven wrong. "He prepares a table before me in the presence of my enemies" Psalm 23:5. No one can stop you from success unless you allow them by making you believe you can't. Focus on yourself. Don't compare yourself to someone else. It doesn't give you fulfillment because you never really know what someone else is going through from day to day. They may smile and laugh and seen so successful, but you don't know what's their story. Everyone has untold stories they don't discuss with no one. It would not add on to your happiness comparing yourself. No one person is better or less than the next person. Being humble is essential to your being and living. "He that is faithful in the which is least is also faithful also in much: and he that is unjust in the least is unjust also in much." Luke 16:10

Love

Love is showed through an action for yourself and another, not when it is convenient to show when you love. Most have never really enjoyed because they think love is saying it with words or when gifts being given. But, as soon as you don't do those things, they think and feel like its not love. When you have relationships you may assume, they must make you feel better about yourself but, no one needs to tell you how to love yourself. Your insecurities will not go away from someone being with you and showing you, that they love you. Because you still don't know how to love and enjoy yourself. Those insecurities will always be there. If you don't know what you want, don't expect anyone else to tell you. If you're not happy with yourself, it will be hard for someone to make you happy.

Because your first love is, loving who you are and if you don't know how to love who you are then everyone who tries to love you. Will get hurt by you. Love is patient. When you think things are not happening for you fast enough, you must learn to trust that in the right timing things will work in your favor. Have patience with others because everyone has other things going on in their lives that they must do for themselves. Love is kind. You are being kind to yourself considering your well-being with the choices and decisions you make every day. Consider other people feelings. "Do to others as you would have them do to you" Luke 6:31. Love does not envy; nothing another person has would make you question your self-worth. It does not boast, your possessions or private static doesn't cause you to brag or feel higher than another; it is not proud. It does not dishonor others, and it is not self-seeking. It is not easily angered, and it keeps no record of wrongs. Once you have forgiven yourself or someone, you don't keep reminding yourself of what you did or what that person has done. Love does not delight in evil. It rejoices with the truth. It always protects, keeping safe from harm's way; it still trusts given you strength and believes in you. It still hopes, in adversity love is your power to know things will get better for you, so love perseveres. Love never fails. The love I have in my heart for people is not measured by convenience. It's what of service can I do for you. Because I love it, and it doesn't matter if you don't give me the same in return. I am secure and stable in everything I say, said, do and done. No one is subjected to being criticized or judged by me. Because I am who I am, and we have all have had difficulties and I am still learning. Don't be down on yourself thinking just because a relationship didn't work; it was your fault. It is not your fault. I used to feel like it was my fault when something didn't work out, or an argument occurred. If you were genuine, true to yourself and did your best for someone that's all that matters, don't punish yourself, that relationship that ended has nothing to do with you but more so to do with them. People battle with themselves and sabotage good friendships and relationships all the time. They often reflect their insecurities off on you, like you're the problem. But it is not you, and it never was about you, so don't think why they did what they did to you. They will have to figure that out themselves. You can't try to fix a person because of their past heartache they must learn to heal themselves.

When you're in a relationship that is not growing and your waiting for that person, leave. They will drag you alone, and it will be full of wasted years and tears. Move on with your life; don't hinder yourself feeling resentment for them when they have hurt you. Send them well wishes, let your last words be to them is. I forgive you. They need to hear that more than you think because when someone doesn't know how to love they hurt other people and it's something they have not forgiven themselves for. Hurt people hurt people. Believe once you are moved on, they will realize the right person you were to them. They will need you. Don't feel rejected. You are good enough. You are beautiful. You are valued. Your life is meaningful. And you are the best at what you do, and you are unique, no one can compare. There is no other like you. You got this. Smile go do something for yourself that you love and makes you feel good. Put all your focus on you because of the creation of manifesting starts with you.

Best friend

Sometimes we think being in a committed relationship will solve all our problem of heartache we had in our past. It doesn't. When your starting in a new relationship most of your old insecurities will be brought forth. Because you're scared of being hurt. And that's why most

relationships don’t last because there is arguing, fussing, insecurities, fighting, secrets, and cheating. It would not always be flowers of roses being with someone. The misconception of love is that things will still be good, and you would be in love with that person. The truth is love will show your strength and weakness. Your partner is either going to provoke your power or provoke your weakness. Those are the make and break moments in your relationships. You’re not going to always be in love but the question you must ask yourself, do I stay? Or do I go and start all over with someone new? The truth is we are all dealing with flaws we think we have. We try to love another but haven't even enjoyed ourselves.
We give and give but at what cost. You may have given someone your time for 3 hours straight but haven’t even given yourself time to relax or did something you wanted to do for yourself. You may have told someone you love them but haven't looked in the mirror and said I love you to yourself. You may give someone advice but haven't listened to your own, and that Indicates you don't trust yourself. And, you may have given someone money to do something but haven’t bought yourself anything in a while or walk pass the shoes you want because they were too expensive. What I’m trying to get you to understand is until you become your best friend. You will always have a difficult time in the relationships you decide to have.

No one can become something you're not to yourself. No one can love you until you love yourself. No one can make you happy until your happy with who you are. You can not get anything without vibrating at the frequency you want to attract. It is created inward out not outward in. You can't understand what you want looking outward to fulfill inward.

The truth

In search of the truth look within. You can't find the truth for yourself in others. Assumptions ruin the truth. Because you assume without asking and knowing. When you want to know the truth about a situation look at yourself and examine how you are looking at the situation first. Are you looking at it to justify yourself or action? Is it out of making yourself feel good because not all truth feels right and have happy endings! But whatsoever you do live your truth. Living truth gives you a feeling of your real being of wholeness. When you live your truth insecurities cannot find you. Because uncertainties are only there to hide from the truth when denial is not present. So, live your life in your reality so that no one can call you out and blame you. To cover themselves from the truth.

May you be guided in your journey of life. You have a decision, you either follow your path or be led into following others. Remember you are loved and needed here.

Thank you for reading.

God, Bless

Made in the USA
Columbia, SC
03 June 2019